The Proper Guide to Parlor Games

THE REGENCY REFERENCE SERIES
BOOK ONE

HOLLI JO MONROE

Christell

Party Hard!

From Idaho to Alberta!

Copyright © 2022 by Brillig Press

All rights reserved.

No part of this book may be reproduced in any form or by any electronic or mechanical means, including information storage and retrieval systems, without written permission from the author, except for the use of brief quotations in a book review.

To Karen, you have all the best ideas.

Contents

1. INTRODUCTION	1
How to Use This Book	3
Limits of this Book	4
2. ENTERTAINMENT IN THE REGENCY	5
General Entertainments	6
The More The Merrier	8
3. ENTERTAINMENTS AT HOME	9
4. READING ALOUD	10
What Was Read	12
Including Readings in Your Party	13
Note for Writers	13
5. MUSICAL PERFORMANCES	15
What Was Performed	17
Including Music in Your Party	18
Note for Writers	19
6. DANCING	20
Including Dancing in Your Party	22
7. A NOTE ON REFRESHMENTS	23
Tea and Coffee	23
Other Drinks	24
Savory Foods	25
Sweet Foods	26
Cold Foods	26
8. DRESSING THE PART	28
A Short Fashion Primer	28
Characteristics of Female Dress	31
Characteristics of Male Dress	35

9. CARD GAMES	38
Note for Writers	41
10. SPECULATION	42
Play	43
End	44
Variations	44
11. LOO	45
Limited Five-Card Loo	46
Play	46
End	47
Variations	48
12. LOTTERY	49
Play	50
End	51
Variations	51
13. COMMERCE	52
Play	53
End	54
Variations	54
14. RIDDLES	55
Note for Writers	56
Riddles	56
Conundrums	58
Charades	59
Riddle Answers	61
15. PARLOR GAMES BASICS	63
How They Are Different	65
Crying Forfeits	65
Including Parlor Games in Your Game Night	66
16. PARLOR GAMES	68
Don't Laugh Games	69
Memory Games	71

Acting Games	75
Blindfolded Games	81
Guessing Games	87
Kissing Games	91
Active Games	95
Word Games	99
17. CRYING FORFEITS	104
How it Works	105
Suggested Penances	107
18. ADDITIONAL RESOURCES	112
Literature	113
Recommended Short Poems	117
Music	119
Recipes	123
White Soup	125
Chicken Salad	127
Negus	129
Syllabub	131
Ices	133
More Riddles	137
More Riddle Answers	145
19. ENJOYED THIS BOOK?	147
Join the Inner Circle Newsletter	147
Acknowledgments	149
About the Author	151
Selected Bibliography	153

Introduction

"One half of the world cannot understand the pleasures of the other."

— EMMA

Just over 200 years ago, King George III sat on the throne of the United Kingdom of Great Britain, and Ireland. But due to his declining mental health, his son George, the Prince of Wales, ruled as a Regent. His Regency lasted from 1811–1820 and gave birth to the name used to identify this period of history. The years 1795–1837 are classified by historians as the Regency (or Long Regency). This transition period between the Georgian Age and Victorian Age is the focus of this book.

THE PRINCE REGENT

The average person knows little about the events or people of the Regency but will recognize the name Jane Austen. In fact, some of the most well-known people from the Regency aren't people but characters in Austen's novels. This longevity and cultural saturation is a testament to her talent and skill. She has reached the kind of immortality that very few artists achieve.

Like many others, Jane Austen is how I discovered the Regency world and the reason I fell in love with it. But she is not the only writer to make the period come alive for me. Today, novels set between 1795 and 1837 are considered historical fiction, but Austen was writing about the world and society she lived in.

Her characters were drawn from her family and neighbors, the settings combinations of visited places and her imagination. When she writes her characters playing whist, she expected her readers to know the game. Like a modern writer referencing a meme or pop culture, her audience was meant to recognize a reference to a bawdy riddle. Unfortunately, with more than 200 years between us, the modern audience is sometimes left in the dark.

One of the goals of the Regency Reference Series is to illuminate some of that darkness. My hope is that these books will help readers have a new understanding of this fascinating era. However, this is not the only goal. I also want people to have fun!

This book is full of entertainments common in the Regency. It is designed to act as a handbook for throwing a Regency Game Night. Though these entertainments are old, they can still be enjoyed today.

There are several ways to connect to the past and enjoying the same pastimes is one of the most genuine. Many of the activities in this book predate the Regency by hundreds of years. How incredibly human to play a game that is perhaps a thousand years old?

HOW TO USE THIS BOOK

This book's primary purpose is as a guide for a Regency-themed party. However, I believe it will also be useful for those interested in this aspect of Regency life or as a research tool for fellow authors. In a few places, I have included asides for writers. For readability, I have included an "Additional Resources" section. Longer explanations and helpful information can be found here. For further research, I have also included a selected bibliography.

LIMITS OF THIS BOOK

This is by no means a complete account of all the entertainments in the early nineteenth century. I am not diving into children's games or activities outside the home, such as attending the theatre or local fairs.

This book focuses on entertainments that could be accomplished at home with small groups of people. It will concentrate primarily on the more active parlor games with some attention given to card games and riddles.

To guide you in your party planning, it will also provide general information on other entertainment, refreshments, and clothing.

While my references include primary sources and scholarly books, this is not an academic treatise. My sole intent is to help people immerse themselves more fully in the Regency.

Entertainment in the Regency

Well, mother, I have done something for you that you will like. I have been to the theatre, and secured a box for tomorrow night. A'n't I a good boy? I know you love a play; and there is room for us all.

— PERSUASION

AN ENDURING ASPECT OF ALL HUMANITY IS OUR ability to seek out entertainment. Today much of our amusements involve screens, but in the Regency era, they involved being in a room with other people—watching them, listening to them, or interacting in a game. Even reading, something most of us consider a solitary activity, was often done as a group.

GENERAL ENTERTAINMENTS

For those rich enough to have leisure time and fortunate enough to live in London, Bath, or other cities, their entertainment would include going out to various venues.

For plays, pantomimes, acrobatics, or operas they would have attended a purpose-built theatre. Musical performances were often held at regular times in public buildings such as the Assembly Rooms in Bath or in churches. Similarly, academic lectures were often hosted in assembly rooms or on the campus of a university or hospital. There were also museums, pleasure gardens, menageries, art galleries, and traveling exhibitions.

Additionally, there were amusements that have fallen out of fashion over the centuries. We no longer visit mental institutions or marvel at freak shows. Blood sports that involved animals are rare today but common then.

Baiting dogs, badgers, bulls, or other animals could

provide an afternoon's enjoyment. Bear baiting was less common, however, not because the population objected to the practice, but because the importation of bears had become difficult due to wars. Cock-fighting was also popular and special cock-pits were a big attraction. Many of these London-based amusements will be covered in more detail in the second book in this series, *The Proper Guide to Regency London*.

Just like today, country life was quieter but had the advantage of providing opportunities for outdoor activities like hunting, fishing, or shooting. People also amused themselves with contests of strength or team sports like cricket or football (soccer to Americans). Many of the London entertainments could be enjoyed on a limited basis through traveling theatre troupes, menageries, or exhibitions. Cock-fighting was unfortunately found across the country in many public houses.

But, just like today, many people spent their nights at home.

THE MORE THE MERRIER

At-home activities might occur with only the family, but more often friends and neighbors were invited to attend dinner or an evening party. In a time when travel was a more complicated and trying undertaking, it was common for people to visit their friends or family for extended periods of time

In *Pride and Prejudice,* we see Darcy on long visits to Netherfield and Rosings. When he returns home to Pemberley, he is accompanied by Bingley and his sisters who are now the visitors. During the novel, three of the Bennet sisters leave home for long periods—London, Kent, and Brighton. With the exception of Emma Woodhouse, every Austen heroine has an extended absence from home visiting friends or family.

Something that was common at the time but completely absent from Austen's novels is a house party. This omission might be because few of Austen's characters had enough money for such an undertaking. A proper house party required a large estate because the host would need to shelter not just their guests but their servants and horses. The guest list might contain twenty to thirty people. Keeping that many people fed and entertained for a month could cost around two thousand pounds. That's Mr. Bennet's yearly income.

In my book, *The Imagined Attachment,* the hero, Sir Phillip, throws a small house party to help his brother get married. Part of the fun of that book was researching what kind of entertainment they might enjoy each night. A large part of that research has gone into this book.

So when you plan your Regency evening, to make it truly authentic you need to invite some friends! Luckily, they won't bring their horses and you only need to feed them for one evening.

Entertainments At Home

Ah! There is nothing like staying at home for real comfort. Nobody can be more devoted to home than I am.

— EMMA

THE ACTIVITIES FOUND WITHIN THE CONFINES OF A drawing room are simpler but perhaps more familiar. A family member performing a song or telling a story is a more universal experience than attending a Regency era opera. These types of at-home entertainments are what filled Jane Austen's life and her novels. One of the reasons her stories endure is because we can all relate to sitting around a dinner table or playing a card game.

While this book will cover card games and parlor games at length, these were not the only entertainments that might be enjoyed in the evenings. For an authentic Regency night you might consider adding any of the following pastimes.

Reading Aloud

THE ORIGINAL AUDIOBOOK

> The person, be it gentleman or lady, who has not pleasure in a good novel, must be intolerably stupid.
>
> — NORTHANGER ABBEY

Long before professional narrators and recording booths, there was the practice of reading aloud. This could be done at any time of the day with anywhere from one listener to an entire room. Primary sources of the time are littered with references to listening to someone read. Every Austen novel mentions the practice and several include scenes with reading being the main activity.

In addition to providing group entertainment, reading aloud was also economical. On a dark evening, it would be very expensive to light enough candles for an entire room to read. A single reader meant less light was needed and less money was spent.

Being a good reader was an attractive quality in a potential spouse. It provided entertainment and allowed the listeners to discern the reader's feelings and tastes.

In *Sense and Sensibility*, Marianne is appalled at Edward Ferrars's inability to read with proper passion and prefers Willoughby's reading. In *Mansfield Park*, Edmund Bertram and Henry Crawford talk at length about the importance of acquiring the skill and bemoan how few acquired it.

The clergymen in particular needed to be able to read well since it was part of their profession. All of Austen's clergymen have some talent for reading to others, although Mr. Collins turns up his nose at reading novels and Mr. Tilney has a tendency to start reading silently so he can finish the book faster.

Being a good reader did not mean the man was pious or a desirable match. Like Willoughby, Henry Crawford has a particular talent for reading aloud; "in Mr. Crawford's reading there was a variety of excellence beyond what she had ever met with." Henry likely knew that a suitor could endear himself to his intended through his reading like Robert Martin did with Harriet Smith or Captain Benwick with Louisa Musgrove.

Of course, reading was not just done by men. One of Fanny Price's duties is to read to her aunt and reading a novel together was often done among friends and family. Sharing the ups and downs of a novel with a group could enhance the experience. Much like a book club today.

She could not abstract her mind five minutes; she was forced to listen; his reading was capital, and her pleasure in good reading extreme.

— MANSFIELD PARK

WHAT WAS READ

The material varied based on the needs of the party and the strength of the reader. One might share something short like a recently received letter, a newspaper article, or some verses of poetry. Longer volumes would be read over several days or, if the weather was particularly bad and the evening long, they might finish it in a day.

Types of longer reading might include novels, plays, epic verse, religious lectures, memoirs, travelogs, or educational nonfiction. Mr. Collins chose to read *Fordyce's Sermons* while Willoughby read *Hamlet* and Tilney read the gothic novel *The Mysteries of Udolpho*.

Of course, not all books were considered suitable for reading in company--the bawdy and sexually explicit novels *Tom Jones* or *Tristram Shandy* would certainly be read silently.

INCLUDING READINGS IN YOUR PARTY

No matter how authentic, I doubt many of your friends would prefer to sit around and listen to each other read all night. However, you could pick a short passage to be read aloud at the beginning of the party, perhaps while people are eating their refreshments.

The easiest option would be to choose a favorite passage from Austen. The famous opening of *Pride and Prejudice* or the last chapter of *Persuasion* would do nicely. Or you might even pick one of her lesser-known poems.

But I think it might be more entertaining to opt for something that was popular at the time. A short poem might be easiest to fit into the night's activities. In my book, *The Imagined Attachment*, they read from a collection by William Wordsworth. But something by Samuel Coleridge, William Cowper, John Keats, Lord Byron, or William Blake would also be appropriate. See Additional Resources for recommended poems and a list of literature mentioned in Jane Austen's writing.

If nobody in your company is brave enough to read, you could play an audiobook or dramatic reading. YouTube and LibriVox are full of high-quality options.

NOTE FOR WRITERS

Reading aloud can be used in a variety of ways. Through their choice of reading material, a character might display their personality or their romantic sensibilities (or lack thereof). In *Sense and Sensibility*, Willoughby's choice of *Hamlet* is clever foreshadowing since he abandons Marianne much like Hamlet abandons Ophelia.

Reading a novel together on a rainy day can provide your main couple with more time in each other's presence. Additionally, reading a book together might bond two characters and give them shared reference points. There is lots of amazing literature to choose from, if one looks beyond Lord Byron or Fanny Burney.

In my book, *The Imagined Attachment*, Daniel, the charming younger brother, is an excellent reader. His ability is a source of jealousy for Phillip, his elder brother. Daniel's reading brings out Phillip's feelings of inadequacy while also highlighting Daniel's personality. His choice of Wordsworth reveals deeper sensitivity than he displays in regular conversation.

Musical Performances

OR THE REGENCY TALENT SHOW

"It will be her turn soon to be teased," said Miss Lucas. "I am going to open the instrument, Eliza, and you know what follows."

"You are a very strange creature by way of a friend!—always wanting me to play and sing before anybody and everybody! If my vanity had taken a musical turn, you would have been invaluable; but as it is, I would really rather not sit down before those who must be in the habit of hearing the very best performers."

On Miss Lucas's persevering, however, she added, "Very well, if it must be so, it must." And gravely glancing at Mr. Darcy, "There is a fine old saying, which everybody here is of course familiar with: 'Keep your breath to cool your porridge'; and I shall keep mine to swell my song."

— PRIDE AND PREJUDICE

One evening at Netherfield, Mr. Darcy, Miss Bingley, and Elizabeth discuss the qualities of an accomplished woman. In addition to other things, Miss Bingley claims that such a woman "must have a thorough knowledge of music and singing."

Being accomplished in many talents added to a woman's value in the marriage mart. But there was a practical reason for this requirement since a musician in the family also helped pass the long hours. On any given evening, a woman might be called upon to entertain those gathered in the drawing room with an impromptu performance.

Most young women would pick pieces that displayed their skills or vocal range. These pieces would be practiced repeatedly so they could be performed at a whim. Ability levels varied and it was best to choose a song that did not stretch one's talent too far. It was also preferable to choose a song that the audience would enjoy. This might be an old favorite, a recent popular song, or something new that nobody had heard.

Musical entertainment was not limited to women giving solo performances on pianofortes. Men with musical talent would also be put on display. They might perform individually or sing a duet like Frank Churchill did with Emma and Jane Fairfax. Violins, flutes, cellos, oboes, harps, and other instruments could be played in a solo or part of an ensemble.

While any night would contain some musical entertainment, a party could also be given with musical performances as its main objective. Those in attendance would come with the understanding that the night would be filled with music.

Wealthy people could hire famous foreigners to perform for their guests. An Italian singer or a German piano player would make for a memorable evening. Alternatively, the guests themselves could take turns performing in a kind of talent show.

WHAT WAS PERFORMED

Thousands of new songs were printed every year. Sheet music was sold in stores and on the streets. Ballad singers would entice buyers by singing the songs while they walked the streets. Often this was the only way to learn the tune as the broadsheets contained only the lyrics. Friends would also exchange sheet music, loaning them to each other so they could make copies and add them to their books. The eight-volume collection of Jane Austen's sheet music owned by the Chawton House Trust is largely written in Austen's handwriting.

Unlike today, the boundary between classical and popular music was indistinct. A piano sonata by Haydn would be played alongside an Irish or Scotch air, followed by a ballad from a popular opera, and a lively dance tune. While some music was purely instrumental, many included lyrics. These ranged from serious to hilarious, sentimental to bawdy, patriotic to religious. They might tell a story, evoke strong emotions, be designed to show off musical ability, or tell jokes.

In her novels, Austen rarely used specifics when referencing music, preferring instead to describe the type of music instead of naming a specific song. She never mentions famous composers of her time like Mozart, Beethoven, or Schubert. The only named piece of music is an Irish tune played by Jane Fairfax in *Emma* called "Robin Adair."

INCLUDING MUSIC IN YOUR PARTY

If you are musically inclined, you might put on a small performance for your guests. You could also ask them to prepare their own musical numbers and have a musicale. The Additional Resources section contains a list of songs and links to sheet music from the period.

Given how modern people are not as accustomed to such performances, it might be difficult to recruit your guests. Alternatively, you can create a playlist to be played in the background during the party. The Additional Resources section will help you in building an excellent one.

It is perfectly acceptable to also play soundtracks from your favorite Austen adaptations. Just be aware that some music used in these movies and mini-series are widely inaccurate to the time period. In some cases, songs that had been out of style for a hundred years are used in ball scenes. Of course, for most of us these soundtracks evoke the Regency and so authenticity might need to be sacrificed to obtain the proper party ambiance.

NOTE FOR WRITERS

Austen used the performing of music to signal many things about her characters. What instrument one plays, how they play, what music they choose, how often they practice, and when they play can all be significant. The possibilities are almost endless.

Having a performance introduces additional opportunities. Who can forget Frank Churchill's duet with Emma and then Jane Fairfax? Or Elizabeth Bennet scolding Mr. Darcy using piano playing as a metaphor? If your character plays an instrument, use it to deepen their personality and convey information to the reader.

In *The Imagined Attachment*, the musical evening gave the hero and heroine a chance to connect while also highlighting the heroine's economic circumstances and personality. Elaine, the heroine, learned to play easy, lively songs at school but now back home she has no instrument. She must perform having not practiced on an instrument. Her nerves are calmed by the hero in one of my favorite scenes.

Dancing

Mr. Darcy stood near them in silent indignation at such a mode of passing the evening, to the exclusion of all conversation, and was too much engrossed by his thoughts to perceive that Sir William Lucas was his neighbor, till Sir William thus began:

"What a charming amusement for young people this is, Mr. Darcy! There is nothing like dancing after all. I consider it as one of the first refinements of polished society."

"Certainly, sir; and it has the advantage also of being in vogue amongst the less polished societies of the world. Every savage can dance."

— PRIDE AND PREJUDICE

During the Regency, dancing was not limited to private balls or public assembly rooms. An afternoon might be pleasantly passed by practicing steps or learning a new dance. Dinner parties could end with rolling up the carpet and enjoying a few country dances. This occurs in several Austen novels but most famously at Sir William Lucas's home where

Mr. Darcy utters one of his more quotable lines: "every savage can dance."

At the time most would have agreed with Sir William that dancing was a "charming amusement." Dancing was considered a healthy form of exercise and a dance after dinner was a good way to work off a meal.

Since many of the dances required a great deal of moving and skipping, the ability to participate in an evening of dance indicated a healthy constitution. Fanny Price in *Mansfield Park* grows quite winded at the ball thrown in her honor. Being a graceful and skillful dancer was an admirable quality and generally desired in a partner (both in life and on the dance floor).

After dinner, dances would be accompanied by an obliging member of the party. This was another reason for a young lady to hone her piano skills, although an unmarried young lady who plays instead of dances is a sure mark that she is less desirable or "on the shelf." At the Lucas's it is Mary that provides the music. In *Persuasion,* the "office of musician" falls to Anne and serves to highlight her separation from the Musgrove family and Captain Wentworth.

A full explanation of how to perform Regency dances

could fill an entire book. For the curious, there are several useful references in the Selected Bibliography.

INCLUDING DANCING IN YOUR PARTY

At the end of the festivities, you could turn your playlist to a particularly energetic song and invite your guests to do their best impression of a Regency dance. You might also employ an instructor knowledgeable about period dances and have them teach one to your guests. Or go online and find a few instructional videos to play and practice with the group.

A Note on Refreshments

> Sir John never came to the Dashwood's without either inviting them to dine at the Park the next day, or to drink tea with them that evening.
>
> — SENSE AND SENSIBILITY

ALL EVENINGS OF MERRIMENT SHOULD CONTAIN some kind of refreshment and a good host would be sure to provide handsomely for their guests. While this book will not instruct you on how to host a Regency dinner party, it will provide some information on common foods served in the period that would be appropriate for your party. The Additional Resources section provides recipes for some of the food and drink mentioned below.

TEA AND COFFEE

While many guests would come for dinner and stay the whole evening, others might be invited just for the entertainment portion of the night. In general, those not invited to dinner were not as highly esteemed as those who were.

When Emma Woodhouse attends the Cole's party, she is invited to dine but her friend Harriet Smith joins that party after dinner. While latecomers won't receive a meal, they would be offered some refreshments. Tea and coffee were the staples of an evening's provisions. Unlike today, tea was a luxury good that high-income families would keep under lock and key. Because of the expense, tea was made weak with a good deal of milk and sugar added. Coffee was primarily enjoyed by upper and middle-class people, but its quality and preparation varied widely.

OTHER DRINKS

In addition to tea and coffee you could offer your guests other popular drinks of the period. The non-alcoholic included lemonade and orgeat. Orgeat is an almond-flavored orange syrup that would be added to water and can still be purchased in many grocery stores today.

Alcoholic drinks tended to be sweeter with Madeira wine and ratafia being highly favored. Ratafia is a cordial or liqueur flavored with nuts or fruits. Its alcohol content varied.

In the early hours of a winter ball, negus might be offered to the guests. Negus is a mix of port wine with sugar, hot water, lemon, and spices. In *Mansfield Park*, Fanny ends her ball feeling "feverish with hopes and fears, soup and negus."

Syllabub was a favorite of Austen's. It is a sweet alcoholic drink known for its frothy, creamy top. Made with cream, egg whites, white wine, sugar, and lemons, it ranged from a creamy dessert to a thinner beverage depending on its preparation. The wine could be replaced with apple cider. In the Regency, this would have been mildly alcoholic but you can make it with unfermented cider.

SAVORY FOODS

If you feel you must provide some kind of meal for your guests, a good option would be a light soup. Soup was generally served at private balls. Mr. Bingley served white soup at Netherfield, and it also makes an appearance at balls held in Highbury and Mansfield Park. It was a variety of soup reserved for wealthy families because it contained expensive ingredients —cream, almonds, and egg yolks.

Other Regency-appropriate foods include cold cuts of meat, cheeses, lettuce and cucumber salad, and a variety of nuts. Toast or muffins was also commonly served with tea and coffee.

SWEET FOODS

Fruit was often served for dessert. Grapes, peaches, apricots, raspberries, and plums were all widely available during the Regency. More exotic fruits, like pineapple, were very expensive and only served at the best parties. Remember that in the early eighteenth century there were no refrigerators and fruit was served cooked, dried, candied, or jellied (not jam but molded gelatin). With few exceptions, they were not served fresh. The traditional Christmas plum pudding is a good example of a cooked fruit dish.

Custards, pastries, and cakes would also be served. But their variety and types could fill their own book.

COLD FOODS

Colder foods, like ices, will help to cool down your guests after the more strenuous games. Ices were essentially ice cream or sorbet, though less sweet than our modern version and containing more interesting flavors. Recipes from 1770 include such flavors as jasmine, celery, ginger, elderflowers, avocado, pineapple, eggplant, barberries, and white coffee. For an authentic Regency experience, you might put the ice cream into a mold. Fruit shapes were common but animals and plants were also used. These would be garnished to give the appearance of a real fruit or plant.

Hopefully you now have some ideas for what kind of food you would like to serve at your Regency Game Night. Before providing spirits, consider the effect they might have on your merry-making. But remember that drinking heavily was not uncommon in the Regency and might just add to the authenticity of the night!

Dressing the Part

PROPER REGENCY ATTIRE

"Do you understand muslins, sir?"

"Particularly well; I always buy my own cravats, and am allowed to be an excellent judge; and my sister has often trusted me in the choice of a gown..."

— NORTHANGER ABBEY

WHILE IT IS PERFECTLY ACCEPTABLE TO ENJOY YOUR Regency party in regular clothes, it must be said that dressing for the occasion can be half the fun! To dress the part, you might modify clothes you already own, hunt down something in a thrift store, buy a ready-made outfit, or have one custom made. There are many talented seamstresses that specialize in Regency attire that offer clothing at various price points.

A SHORT FASHION PRIMER

The Regency has a distinctive clothing style that, thanks to the many Austen adaptations, makes it instantly recognizable even to the average modern individual. It marked a transition period between the wigs and width of the Georgian period and the buttoned-up Victorian period. The overall aesthetic was one of drawing inspiration from the past, particularly from Ancient Greece and Rome.

Classicism was the major influence during the Regency, with many styles mimicking ancient statues and drawings. Ornamentation was discarded for a more streamlined naturalism. Fashion tended to favor the slim, plain, and proportional to the body.

What was worn could vary based on season, time of day, or activity. I will be focusing on evening dress that would be suitable for wearing to a dinner party. I will not be discussing period appropriate undergarments such as stays, shifts, or stockings, though you might be interested to know that a proper Regency lady did not wear underwear like we have today. So if you want to be truly authentic, you should consider going commando.

However you achieve your Regency look, make sure you are comfortable and can move freely. Many of the parlor games require movement, and we wouldn't want any wardrobe mishaps!

Characteristics of Female Dress

How do you like Jane's hair? You are a judge. She did it all herself. Quite wonderful how she does her hair! No hairdresser from London I think could.

— EMMA

CLOTHING

A key characteristic of the Regency look is the waistline. During Jane Austen's life, waistlines rose from near the natural waist to just below the bust. The waistline rose as high as a mere two and a half inches from the neckline, but there is no need to go that far in your own costume. Today an under bust waistline is known as an empire waist, named after the French First Empire period (1804-15).

The hemline was to the floor and the bodice a single straight tube, mimicking a long column. The sleeves were generally short caps with various amounts of volume at the shoulder. A longer, gauzy sleeve did come back into fashion in the 1810s. You can get a good sense of period clothing by searching the internet for portraits of the time or fashion museums for their collections.

Modern fashionistas declare that all women should own a little black dress, but in the Regency, the simple white dress was a fashion staple. Any woman in the gentry class or above would have owned at least one white muslin gown. When putting together your own outfit, you can't go wrong with a white dress.

ACCESSORIES

In the evenings, white kid gloves were worn above the elbow and ribbons could be used to tie them in place. Shoes would be flat-soled slippers in a satin or silk that coordinated with the dress. Although bonnets were not worn in the evening, some might choose an evening cap or turban to complement their outfit. A fan or modest jewelry will complete your ensemble.

For those who get chilly, a large rectangular shawl may also be added.

HAIR

Unlike the powdered style of a decade earlier, Regency ladies had clean, natural hair. The back hair was left long while the front was cut close around the face. The back hair was most often worn up off the neck and the front hair was curled to mimic the Grecian or Roman style.

Women with naturally curly hair were lucky; those with straight hair used papers to curl them at night. Various adornments might be woven through the hair: beads, ribbons, fabric, or flowers. Proper Regency hair requires a second person to create a complex design in the back. Someone like Jane Fairfax, who could do her hair on her own, was most likely too poor to afford a maid.

Powdered wigs were a thing of the past, but wigs in a natural hair color were often used. These might augment someone's natural hair or cover their head entirely. A wig could be purchased at a shop, created from the person's own hair, or donated by a willing family member. Some women were known to wear a hat covering their head and a small hairpiece that would stick out of the cap to give the illusion of full hair.

MAKEUP

The natural look was most prized by respectable society. Using cosmetics to hide flaws was a disapproved practice. Instead, lotions and creams were encouraged to improve complexion. Rouge and powder were acceptable.

> I should recommend Gowland, the constant use of Gowland, during the spring months. Mrs. Clay has been using it at my recommendation, and you see what it has done for her. You see how it has carried away her freckles.
>
> — PERSUASION

Characteristics of Male Dress

"But he talked of flannel waistcoats," said Marianne; "and with me a flannel waistcoat is invariably connected with the aches, cramps, rheumatisms, and every species of ailment that can afflict the old and the feeble."

— SENSE AND SENSIBILITY

CLOTHING

The basic male outfit included white linen shirt, a waistcoat, coat, knee-length breeches, and cravat. Often the breeches would be held up by suspenders (or braces). In previous periods waistcoats had tails, but like women's waistlines, the tails rose and were then eliminated completely.

While the waistcoat meets the breeches, the coats contain two tails at the back. The coat was cut in at the waist and the collars were wide and turned back. The ideal figure was one with broad shoulders, small waist, and muscular thighs. Later in the Regency, breeches were joined by pantaloons and trousers. Both were ankle length but the pantaloons were tight and the trousers loose.

Cravats were made of white linen, cotton, or silk and cut into a large square. The square is folded diagonally and wrapped around the neck over the linen shirt collar. These could be tied in a variety of styles and a well-tied cravat was the mark of a gentleman of fashion. To properly achieve the Regency style, the collar of the shirt should touch the cheeks.

Coats were plain colors with no pattern. Evening dress was generally a black coat. Likewise, legwear would be black or cream. Waistcoats could be bright silks or printed cottons and were a chance for men to indulge in something eye-catching.

ACCESSORIES

Men had fewer accessories. A decorative stick pin used to hold their cravat in place or fobbed watch was the extent for most but true dandies might wear more. Hats were not worn in the evening but short leather gloves were. Evening shoes were dark leather pumps with a low, slipper-like profile. A knee-length leather dress boot would also be acceptable. The goal of the footwear was to make the legs appear longer.

HAIR

Like women, hair powder was done away with and a natural look was embraced. Taking cues from classical sculpture, men's hair was cropped shorter than before. Curled and artfully disheveled was preferred. A man who lacked naturally curly hair might also resort to papers. The only acceptable facial hair were side whiskers which grew in fashion throughout the period.

Natural wigs were also used for those whose hair had begun to disappear.

MAKEUP

Cosmetics for men was frowned upon but the more vain might have used lotions or creams. I like to imagine that Sir Walter from *Persuasion* secretly used Gowland's lotion to achieve the complexion he often boasted about.

Card Games

A BRIEF INTRODUCTION

"What shall I do, Sir Thomas? Whist and speculation; which will amuse me most?"

Sir Thomas, after a moment's thought, recommended speculation. He was a whist player himself, and perhaps might feel that it would not much amuse him to have her for a partner.

— MANSFIELD PARK

More sedate games are often featured in Austen's novels. From her letters, we know that she enjoyed cards and was quite proficient. She specifically mentions playing whist, brag, vingt-et-un, casino, speculation, commerce, quadrille, and cribbage. Though some characters in her novels do not seem to care for such games, they were a very common occurrence in drawing rooms of the period.

Often the modern reader connects card playing to gambling and possibly some moral failing, but in the Regency, playing for small sums was normal. Of course, playing for high stakes and losing more than one could afford did present a problem. While high stakes were often found in clubs, one could also lose big in a drawing room.

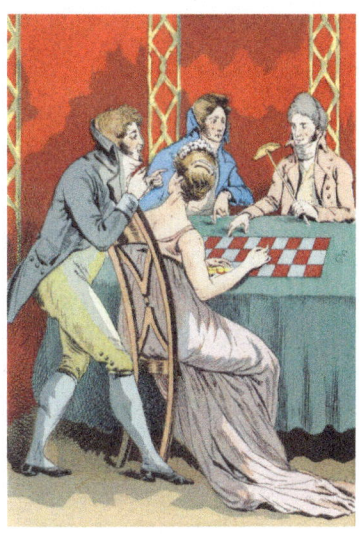

In *Pride and Prejudice* when Elizabeth declines to play at Netherfield, her objection isn't to the gambling but to the fact she suspected "them to be playing high." Perhaps Mr. Hurst was hoping to win some money off his prosperous brother-in-law and his rich friend?

For those who did not wish to play with money, they might use counters instead. These counters could be in any shape and made of metal, wood, ivory, or even mother-of-pearl. This practice is seen in *Pride and Prejudice* where they play the lottery game and Lydia is obsessed with how many fish she won and lost. In this case, the counters were probably shaped like fish, which was a common shape. Those who played regularly would have their own counters and often a bag or box designed specifically to carry them.

Most of the following games require counters. For your party, you might use poker chips, small coins, or ask your friends to bring their own homemade counters. Just know whether you play for money or counters, you will be authentic to the period.

Since this is not a book specific to Regency card games, I will only be including games that can be played with larger groups, so called "round games." For example, whist is not included. Whist was often played at card parties but a game is made up of four people. In order to play it at your party, you would need multiple tables and a deck of cards for each.

Some of these games have modern versions, but I will be using the rules from the 1810 New Pocket Hoyle handbook. This way you can be sure you are playing the same way as Austen and her characters.

"Lydia talked incessantly of lottery tickets, of the fish she had lost and the fish she had won..."

— PRIDE AND PREJUDICE

NOTE FOR WRITERS

Cards are a great way to separate your characters and allow for private conversations in crowded drawing rooms. One can also use the type of game a character prefers or how they play the game to reveal aspects of their personality.

For example, Lydia Bennet being obsessed with her lottery game and how many fish she won or lost says much about her risk-taking nature. Isabella Thorpe enjoying a game of commerce, a game that involves trading cards in an attempt to get a better hand, is a perfect metaphor for her personality.

Speculation

...securing his knave at an exorbitant rate, [Mary Crawford] exclaimed, "There, I will stake my last like a woman of spirit. No cold prudence for me. I am not born to sit still and do nothing. If I lose the game, it shall not be from not striving for it."

— MANSFIELD PARK

SPECULATION IS A NOISY GAMBLING GAME THAT HAS fallen out of fashion in the last hundred years or so. It requires very little attention from the players. They only need to remember what cards have been played.

Materials: a deck of cards, counters for each player
Number of Players: 2 to 9; An additional deck will allow for more players.
Wining the Round: The player possessing the highest trump card after all cards are exposed wins the pot.
Winning the Game: At the end of play, the player with the most counters wins.

PLAY

Everyone begins the game with the same number of counters. At the beginning of each deal an ante is added to a pot in the center. The dealer adds six counters and everyone else adds four.

Each player receives three cards, dealt face down on the table in a stack. They do NOT look at their cards.

After dealing, the dealer turns over the top card on the remaining deck of cards. This card determines the trump suit for the round. The trump suit is the only one that matters to win the game. Aces are high.

If the card turned over is an ace, the dealer automatically wins the round and collects the pot.

If the card is not an ace, players may attempt to use their counters to buy the trump card from the dealer. The dealer can auction the card, trade the card, or keep it.

Play starts to the left of the owner of the trump card. This could be the dealer or the purchaser of the trump card.

Each player turns over their top card in succession.

When a higher trump card is turned over, its owner may sell the card or keep it.

If sold, play resumes to the left of the purchaser.

Players continue to reveal their cards in rotation. The

player with the highest trump card is exempt from showing their card until the end of the round or they no longer have the highest card.

END

The round ends when a trump ace is played or all dealt cards are revealed.

The player with the highest trump card wins the pot of counters. If there are enough cards left in the deck, played cards go into a discard pile.

The next dealer is the player seated to the left of the first dealer.

VARIATIONS

1. During game play, allow players to look at their dealt cards.
2. During game play, allow players to trade dealt cards with other players. Purchasers and sellers may not look at the cards. The traded cards are placed at the bottom of a player's stack and played in the normal course of play.
3. At the beginning of the round, an extra hand is dealt. At the end of the round, the cards are revealed. If the extra hand contains a higher trump than the winners, the pot stays in the center and is added to the next round.

Loo

On entering the drawing-room she found the whole party at loo, and was immediately invited to join them; but suspecting them to be playing high she declined it, and making her sister the excuse, said she would amuse herself for the short time she could stay below, with a book.

— PRIDE AND PREJUDICE

LOO IS A GAME THAT CAME TO ENGLAND BY WAY OF France sometime in the mid-1600's. It was popular as both a harmless parlor game and a more competitive high stakes gambling game. A game of loo can be limited or unlimited and played with three or five cards.

Limited loo keeps the money played into the pot by the losers small and fixed. Unlimited loo requires the payments to equal the amount in the pot. An unlimited loo game can quickly reach very high amounts which could easily bankrupt a player. This aspect led to the game acquiring a bad reputation and contributed to its drop in popularity.

It is no wonder Elizabeth Bennet declined to play.

LIMITED FIVE-CARD LOO

Materials: a deck of cards, counters for each player
Number of Players: 5 to 10
Wining the Round: Take at least one trick.
Winning the Game: Have the most counters at the end.
Card Values: Aces are high.
The Knave of Clubs (or Jack in modern parlance) is called Pam and beats every card in the pack.
A flush is five cards of the same suit or four plus Pam. Highest flush is four plus Pam. The second highest is a flush in the trump suit. The third is a flush in a plain or non-trump suit with the highest value cards.

PLAY

Each player begins with the same number of counters.

The first dealer is chosen by having everyone draw a random card from the deck. The person who draws the lowest card is first dealer.

Play goes to the left.

The round starts with the dealer adding three counters to the pot.

The dealer deals three cards in a batch to each player and then deals two cards in a batch to each player.

Dealer turns over the next card in the deck. This card determines the trump suit.

Players can look at their cards. They can decide to play their hand, exchange any of their cards for new ones (one to five may be exchanged), or choose not to play the round. They announce their decision in turn from the left of the dealer.

Whichever player holds the best flush immediately "looes the board," meaning they win all five tricks without further play. Anyone who does not have Pam or a flush must deposit three counters into the pot.

If there is not a flush, then play begins with the player to the left who lays down a card to start the first trick.

Each player must lay down a card of the same suit. If they have a card higher than the first card, they must play it. If they do not have any cards of that suit, they may lay down any other card.

The trick is taken by the highest card of the same suit as the card that started the trick, or by the highest trump suit if any are played.

The winner of the trick leads the next trick. They must play a trump suit if possible.

If Pam is led, players must play a trump suit card (if they can).

If the trump Ace is played at the start of the trick the player may say "Pam be civil." This means the player holding Pam cannot play it unless they have no other trump suit card.

Play continues until all cards are played.

END

Each trick won earns the player one-fifth of the pot. Any player who does not win a trick must play three counters into the pot. Those who chose not to play the round are exempted.

In the case of a flush, the person with the highest flush takes the entire pot.

VARIATIONS

1. Instead of three counters for each stake, players may agree to a higher or lower standard stake.
2. **Unlimited Loo:** Instead of only adding three counters for not winning a trick, the players must add an amount equal to the size of the pot. For example, if the pot has twenty counters, the players must pay twenty counters each.
3. **Three-Card Loo:** Allows for up to sixteen players. Cards are dealt one at a time. Pam is omitted. There are no flushes. Players must play the hand they are dealt. Cards cannot be exchanged. For each trick won, a player gets one-third of the pot.

Over the years, a more complicated version of Three-Card Loo developed. Since this book is focused on the Regency, I decided to only include the version that is covered in Hoyle's 1810 rule book.

Lottery

Mrs. Philips protested that they would have a nice comfortable noisy game of lottery tickets, and a little bit of hot supper afterwards. The prospect of such delights was very cheering, and they parted in mutual good spirits.

— PRIDE AND PREJUDICE

On the continent, lottery games became popular in the 1500s and then slowly migrated to England. This basic lottery game is easy to play with large groups of people and any age. It is likely this version of the game that was being played when Mr. Wickham shares with Elizabeth his history with Mr. Darcy. Knowing that they were sitting at a card table surrounded by loud play certainly paints their conversation in a different light.

Materials: two decks of cards with different backs to easily differentiate them, counters for each player
Number of Players: 5-40

Winning the Round: Earning counters by matching your ticket card to a prize card.
Winning the Game: Having the most counters at the end of play.

PLAY

One person is designated the manager.

One pack of cards is used for the tickets and one pack is used for the prizes.

Two dealers are chosen in any manner.

Each player puts three counters into the pot (or whatever fixed amount is determined by the manager). This forms the "lottery fund."

After shuffling and cutting the deck, Dealer One gives each player a card. This is their prize card. These cards are dealt face down.

Each player then takes counters from the lottery fund and places them on their prize card. The number of counters is at the discretion of the player.

Dealer Two deals each player a card. This is their ticket card.

The manager orders all cards to be turned over.

Any player whose ticket card matches a prize card wins the counters on the prize card. This ends the round. What constitutes a match is at the discretion of the manager.

The counters on any prize cards that do not have matches are returned to the lottery fund.

All cards are collected, shuffled, and redealt.

When all counters in the fund are used, each player will put three counters into the fund.

END

Game play can end after a designated number of rounds or a specific amount of time or when the lottery fund is depleted.

VARIATIONS

1. Increase or decrease the number of counters required by each player for the fund.
2. Limit the number of counters that can be placed on each prize ticket.
3. Allow players to exchange counters for money at the end of the game.
4. Have players win the counters they placed on their prize card instead of the one that matched their ticket card.

At first there seemed danger of Lydia's engrossing him [Mr. Wickham] entirely for she was a most determined talker; but being likewise extremely fond of lottery tickets, she soon grew too much interested in the game, too eager in making bets and exclaiming after prizes, to have attention for any one in particular.

— PRIDE AND PREJUDICE

Commerce

Catherine was disturbed and out of spirits; but Isabella seemed to find a pool of commerce, in the fate of which she shared, by private partnership with Morland, a very good equivalent for the quiet and country air of an inn at Clifton.

— NORTHANGER ABBEY

Materials: a deck of cards, counters for each player
Number of Players: 3-12
Wining the Round: Have the highest hand when "stop commerce" is called.
Winning the Game: Have the most counters at the end.
Card Values: Aces are elevens. Face cards are ten.
The highest hand is a tricon or three cards of the same denomination, for example, three fives.
The second highest is a sequence of cards in the same suit.
The third highest is two or three cards of the same suit. The higher combined card value wins. If the card value is equal, then three cards beat two cards. If still equal, the player nearest

in turn after the dealer wins. For example, a two, five, and six of clubs would beat an ace and two of hearts.

PLAY

DEALER IS CHOSEN IN ANY MANNER. DEALER IS called "the banker," and the undealt stack of cards "the bank."

At the start of the game each player puts one counter into the pot.

The dealer deals three cards to each player, face down, beginning on the right hand.

If a player receives a face card on the first deal, they will get a fresh deal.

Once all cards are dealt the banker asks, "Who will trade?"

Beginning with the player on the left, the players answer with "For ready money" or "I barter."

If they say "for money," the player gives a card and a counter to the banker. The banker keeps the counter for their pile.

The banker places the card at the bottom of the bank and gives the player a new card from the top of the bank.

If they say "I barter," they exchange one card with the player on their right. The player cannot refuse the trade and neither player gets to choose what card they receive.

Once they have traded, the player must say "done" to end their turn.

Play continues until a player calls "stop the commerce." They may only call a stop during their turn, and a player should only call a stop when they have their desired hand.

A player can choose to call a stop without trading or bartering but must wait for their turn. If the first player calls a stop, nobody will have a chance to trade.

When "stop" is called, all players show their hands. The highest hand wins the pot.

If the banker does not win the pot, they must pay a counter to the player who won.

If the banker has a tricon, sequence, or two or three cards of the same suit but does not win the pot then they give a counter to every player.

END

Play can end when one player has lost all their counters or after a fixed number of rounds.

VARIATIONS

1. Allow players to refuse trades.
2. If a player refuses to trade on their first turn, they are not allowed to trade for the rest of the game.

Riddles

OF VARIOUS TYPES

Mr. Woodhouse was almost as much interested in the business as the girls, and tried very often to recollect something worth their putting in. So many clever riddles as there used to be when he was young—he wondered he could not remember them! but he hoped he should in time.

— EMMA

RIDDLES WERE A POPULAR PASTIME IN THE DRAWING rooms of the Regency. Upper-class women were known to copy them and other interesting examples of the written word into their own collections. In *Emma*, Harriet Smith is engaged in collecting and transcribing "riddles of every sort that she could meet with." She got the idea from one of her teachers who had at least three hundred in her collection. Such collections allowed women to exercise their wit and intelligence.

Since they can easily be included in a Regency game night —and because they are a lot of fun—I have included several in this book. Like Harriet, I have compiled these examples. But instead of quizzing my friends, I have copied them from an eighteenth-century book. They are divided into three different types: riddles, conundrums, and charades.

For your Regency party, you can have a competition for who can answer the most riddles, make them part of the forfeits, or just enjoy sharing them.

Answers are provided at the end of the section. More riddles are located in Additional Resources, along with primary sources for further research. You could also try creating your own or having your party create them together.

NOTE FOR WRITERS

Wordplay was a popular pastime in the Regency and naturally fits into novels. Riddles could be used in a variety of ways. They can display a character's intelligence (or lack thereof) or be the source of a miscommunication or revelation. A well-crafted charade could reveal motives or be used to send a subtle message. Conundrums could add humor or be groan-inducing.

RIDDLES

Most of us are familiar with these kind of word puzzles. They differ from charades and conundrums because they rhyme and can be solved with a one word answer.

Riddle 1
The beginning of eternity the end of time and space
The beginning of every end and the end of ev'ry place

Riddle 2
In the ev'ning I'm long, in the morning I'm small
When seen in a ball room I am nothing at all

Riddle 3
Form'd long ago yet made to day
I'm most in use whilst others sleep
What few would like to give away
And yet what none would wish to keep

Riddle 4
Too much for one enough for two and nothing at all for three

Riddle 5
Destin'd by fate to guard the crown
Aloft in air I reign
Above the monarch's haughty frown
Or statesman's plotting brain
In hostile fields when danger's near
I'm found amidst alarms
In crowds where peaceful beaux appear
I instant fly to arms

CONUNDRUMS

Shorter than a riddle, conundrums are generally only one sentence long. They are a combination of a pun and riddle and involve a play on words. I call them Regency "dad jokes."

Conundrum 1
Why is an empty room like a room full of married people?

Conundrum 2
Why is a clergyman's horse like a king?

Conundrum 3
When a man falls out of the window, what does he fall against?

Conundrum 4
Of what trade is the sun?

Conundrum 5
Why is a handsome woman like bread?

CHARADES

> He called for a few moments, just to leave a piece of paper on the table containing, as he said, a charade, which a friend of his had addressed to a young lady, the object of his admiration, but which, from his manner, Emma was immediately convinced must be his own.
>
> — EMMA

The charade Mr. Elton leaves, is at the heart of a misunderstanding in Austen's *Emma*. Unlike the modern acting version, Regency charades are composite riddles. A word or phrase is cryptically described and the solution involves combining each answer to create a new word.

In Mr. Elton's charade three clues are given. The answer to the first is "court" and the answer to the second is "ship". Combining them makes "courtship."

Mr. Elton submits his clever wordplay to indicate his interest in marrying Emma Woodhouse but it goes awry because she is blinded by her matchmaking.

The following charades are a small selection that can be used in your game night. Or perhaps to initiate a courtship of your own!

Charade 1
My first, whatever be its hue,
Will please, if full of spirit;
My second critics love to do,
And stupid authors merit.

Charade 2
My first opposes you;

My second enriches you:
My whole's the delight of the notable.

Charade 3

My first a man will often take,
In hopes my next to share;
But he who shall possess them both,
Will find them hard to bear.

Charade 4

My first a blessing sent to earth,
of plants and flowers to aid the birth;
My second surely was design'd
To hurl destruction on mankind:
My whole a pledge from pardoning heaven,
Of wrath appeas'd and crimes forgiven.

Charade 5

To a word of consent add one half of a fright;
Next subjoin what you never behold in the night:
These rightly connected, you'll quickly obtain
What numbers have seen but will ne'er see again.

Riddle Answers

RIDDLES

1. Letter E
2. Shadow
3. Bed
4. Secret
5. Hat

CONUNDRUMS

1. there is not a single person in it.
2. A minister directs him.
3. His will.
4. A tanner.
5. She is often toasted.

HOLLI JO MONROE

CHARADES

1. Eyelash
2. Bargain
3. Misfortune
4. Rainbow
5. Yesterday

Parlor Games Basics

> ...hot cockles, questions and commands, and the various modifications of forfeits, ... may do very well for such as are only two or three degrees removed infancy, either in age or intellect.
>
> — THE REPOSITORY OF ARTS, LITERATURE, COMMERCE, (1819)

UNLIKE MANY OF THE GAMES AND AMUSEMENTS previously mentioned, parlor games do not feature in Jane Austen's novels. But thanks to family letters, we know that such games were played in the Austen home. Perhaps she thought the games were beneath the dignity of her characters? Or maybe she saw no narrative use for the games?

One might argue that parlor games were mostly played by younger children and had no place amongst adults. Books written during the period are unclear on the intended age range and many of the games do seem childish. Ackermann's Repository, a contemporary magazine, had an article in 1819 condemning such games when played by adults. But that only proves that adults did play them.

There are many illustrations of the games being enjoyed by all ages. Additionally, the nature of the games seem designed for adult men and women to trespass the bounds of propriety. A game like Blindman's Buff allows a great deal of touching in an environment where it would not normally be permitted. Many of the games involved kissing and contained opportunities to declare feelings.

While these games could be played any time of year, winter —with its long nights and dreary days—was a particularly popular time. Some families might only indulge in parlor games over the winter holidays, particularly during Twelfth Night celebrations when propriety and normalcy were often pushed to their limits.

The games I have included in this book are a small selection of the many that I found in my research. I tried to pick those best suited for modern players. If you are interested, feel free to explore more from the provided primary sources. And if you find one you particularly like, please share it with me!

HOW THEY ARE DIFFERENT

Parlor games are not designed for winning and losing, but for enjoyment. The point of the games is to have fun or to show off your wit. Most of the games do not take long to play and are best enjoyed in combination with each other.

To lead the games, a Master or Mistress of the Revels was appointed. This person needed to be fair, fun-loving, and inventive. It was their duty to manage the evening by picking the games, ensuring rules were followed, keeping track of forfeits, determining when to switch to a new game, and what types of forfeits must be paid. Without a good master or mistress, chaos might ensue, or worse, the night become dull.

Instead of a point system, they used forfeits. For various reasons, a game might result in players paying forfeits to the Master of the Revels. Traditionally these might have been small objects they had on their person—a shilling, a hairpin, a handkerchief, even a cravat—or objects brought specifically to be used for the games. Each forfeit obliges the player to perform a task dictated by the Mistress of the Revels at the end of the night. Paying forfeits could easily be more fun than the actual games. Some games are almost designed to make sure everyone pays a forfeit.

CRYING FORFEITS

At the end of the evening, the Master of the Revels will "cry forfeits," indicating that all forfeits must be redeemed. If players have provided personal items, the only way to retrieve them is by performing their assigned task or "penance." The Master of the Revels ensured they were properly redeemed.

The penance generally requires something silly or ridiculous from the player, like yawning until someone else yawns or making animal sounds. A great many of the suggested forfeits involved kissing. Though authors were quick to note that the kissing could be on the cheek or hand, it seems a "salute" on the lips was common.

A list of suggested forfeits is provided in the Cry Forfeits section.

INCLUDING PARLOR GAMES IN YOUR GAME NIGHT

For your party, choose a Master or Mistress of the Revels. You might fill this role or recruit a friend suited to the position. Before the evening begins, have an idea of what games might be fun to play with your group. Remember that crying forfeits is meant to take up a significant amount of time, so plan accordingly.

You can have your guests pay their forfeits with things they have on their person, counters, or tally them on a sheet of paper. Whatever you choose it is important that they understand what a forfeit is and how it will be redeemed later in the night.

Most importantly, have fun with it! Modify rules as needed and if people are not enjoying a game, change to something else. The point is to laugh and enjoy each other's company.

Note: Words or phrases in quotation marks indicate a direct quote from primary sources.

Parlor Games

DIVIDED BY TYPE

Silly things do cease to be silly if they are done by sensible people in an impudent way.

— EMMA

Don't Laugh Games

The aim of the following games is to get other players to smile or laugh.

THE LAUGHING GAME

All players sit in a circle.
> The first player says, "Ha"
> The second player says, "Ha Ha"
> Third player says, "Ha Ha Ha" and on around the circle.
> If a player laughs or smiles, they are out and pay a forfeit.
> Last one to laugh or smile wins.

POOR KITTY

One player is designated "Kitty."
> "Kitty" kneels in front of a player and meows.
> The player must stroke or pat "Kitty" on the head.

The player must say "Poor Kitty" three times without smiling.

If the player smiles, they pay a forfeit and must become Kitty.

If Kitty cannot get any of the party to smile, they must pay a forfeit.

THE COURTIERS

The "king" or "queen" sit in a chair facing the players.

They perform gestures designed to make the other players laugh.

The other players are "courtiers" and must copy each movement without laughing or smiling.

The first player to laugh earns a forfeit.

The last to laugh becomes the king/queen.

Memory Games

The following games are designed to test the player's memories.

THE DOCTOR

One player is designated "The Doctor."

The Doctor feels each player's pulse, and asks for their "disorder."

The Patient replies with a complaint. Creativity is encouraged!

The Doctor gives them a humorous remedy to match their complaint. It's encouraged to pick something that contrasts with the complaint.

Example:
Patient: I have a fever.
Doctor: Take one snowball every hour.
After the Doctor dispenses the remedies, he will call

on a Patient to remember a particular remedy.

"_____ is ill of _____ complaint. What remedy would you order?"

If the Patient answers incorrectly, they must pay a forfeit.

The game ends after everyone has a chance to answer the Doctor.

THE GAME OF SIGHS

Pick a game leader.

The leader starts the game by saying: "Ladies and gentlemen, it is vain to think of concealing any longer the griefs which are devouring your hearts. You may be permitted to breathe forth those sighs which for want of vent are ready now to suffocate you."

All players begin to sigh and moan.

The leader then asks each person in turn the cause of their afflictions.

Players answer with humorous reasons.

Examples from an 1822 games book:

The cook boiled the rabbits to rags.

Cannot get a man to marry her though she has asked a hundred.

Her mama refused to take her to the bull bait.

Once all the reasons are given, the leader calls on one player to recite their affliction and the affliction of one other player.

That player then recites the two afflictions and adds a third player.

The third owner of the affliction recites the previous three and adds a fourth.

This continues around the circle, getting progressively longer.

Any mistakes earn the player a forfeit.

THE BELLMAN OR HOW TO KEEP A SECRET

One player is the Penitent.

The Penitent takes a player and leads them to the middle of the room.

The Penitent says "I met the bellman now in the marketplace and he told me..."

The Penitent whispers something to the player. Then says aloud, "Now mind you keep it secret for your life, don't tell it to anybody!"

The player says "certainly" and then beckons another player to the center.

The player whispers the secret to the new player. And the new player beckons another player to the center.

Players are called up in turn and told the secret.

Each player then writes their name and the secret on a piece of paper.

If what they write is different from the Penitent's version of the secret, they must pay a forfeit.

Acting Games

These two games encourage players to use their acting skills.

TABLEAUX VIVANTS

Two French words meaning "living picture." This was a very popular pastime in the Regency and beyond. It wasn't so much a game as a chance for people to be creative without doing a full home theatrical. The traditional version of tableaux vivant involved choosing a scene or concept and then building the picture. This was often a complicated endeavor involving full costumes, scenery, and props. People in the neighborhood would then be invited to attend the reveal of the scene. The players would stand motionless while their audience appreciated their artistry.

I love the idea of a tableaux vivant and wanted to include it in *The Imagined Attachment*. Unfortunately, it didn't quite work for my characters or the story. In the end, I decided to do a variation on the concept, that I am including here as the only "original" game in this book.

Create a list of well-known stories and write them on small pieces of paper.

Players pair up, draw a story, and devise a pose using only items on hand.

Each team is given thirty seconds in front of the group.

They perform a pose from their story.

The rest of the group guesses the story on their answer sheet.

The team with the most correct answers wins.

The losing pairs all pay a forfeit.

Possible Stories to Portray

Fairytales

- Sleeping Beauty
- Cinderella
- Snow White
- Little Mermaid
- Beauty and the Beast

Myths and Legends

- King Arthur
- Pandora's Box
- Prometheus
- Hades and Persephone
- Robin Hood

Scriptures

- Garden of Eden
- Noah's Ark
- Parting the Red Sea
- The Nativity
- David and Goliath

PROVERBS IN ACTION

This is very similar to what we now call charades. The major difference is that what is being acted out is limited only to proverbs. During the Regency, shared culture ensured that most people were familiar with the same proverbs. For your game night, it might be easier to have a list of proverbs for people to choose from or write them on slips of paper and have them drawn from a bowl.

A president is chosen. The president's job is to call a vote on the actor's ability and to cast a vote if it is tied.
A player is chosen to be the actor.
The actor chooses a proverb to represent. This can be done from their memory or from a provided list.
The actor begins acting. They are allowed to talk and use props but must not say any words that are in the proverb.

Each player guesses in turn. The actor does not indicate if their guesses are right or wrong. Guessing can be in any order.

After everyone has guessed, the president asks the actor what their proverb is. Every player who guessed wrong earns a forfeit.

If the president deems the acting insufficiently represented the proverb, they will call for a vote.

Every player votes on the actor's representation. If there is a tie, the president will cast the deciding vote.

If the majority felt the acting did not represent the proverb, then the actor receives a forfeit and no other players must pay a forfeit. The actor must then act out a new proverb.

If the proverb was guessed by someone then the actor may sit down and a new actor is chosen.

Players may choose not to act but must pay three forfeits for refusing.

To help, here is an example of how the actor might act out the proverb "a rolling stone gathers no moss."

> "The actor takes a round pebble and rolls it several times up and down the room after which he examines it carefully in all directions and placing a piece of white paper on the table begins to rub the stone with his finger as if trying to detach something from its surface after rubbing some time he holds up the paper to show that there is nothing on it."

Possible Proverbs

- A leopard can't change its spots.
- The apple doesn't fall far from the tree.
- Beggars can't be choosers.
- Don't put all your eggs in one basket.
- Blood is thicker than water.

- It never rains but it pours.
- Curiosity killed the cat.
- Don't cut off your nose to spite your face.
- It's not over till the fat lady sings.
- Once bitten, twice shy.

Blindfolded Games

Many of these games pre-date the Regency. Games like Blindman's Buff or Hot Cockles date back to the Middle Ages. Some variations on these classic games were played in the Regency and are shared here.

BLINDMAN'S BUFF

A blindfolded player is placed in the center of the other players and attempts to touch them.

Once a player is touched by the blindman they are caught.

The caught player must hold still while the blindman tries to determine who they have caught using only their hands.

The blindman gets three guesses. If they guess wrong, they owe a forfeit.

If they guess correctly the caught player becomes the blindman.

SEATED BUFFY

Form a circle with chairs.

All but the blindman sit.

The blindman goes to the center and is blindfolded.

All seated people are commanded to move chairs or the blindman is spun around.

The blindman moves forward until they run into another player.

They then sit on the player's lap and try to guess the person.

The blindman gets three guesses. If they guess wrong, they owe a forfeit.

If they guess correctly then the other player becomes the blindman.

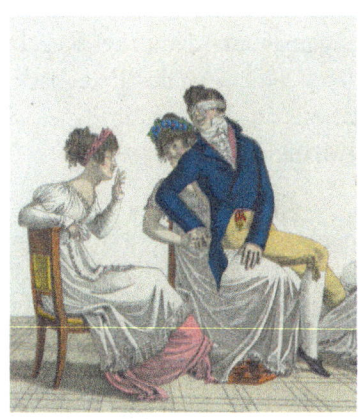

BUFFY GRUFFY

Form a circle of chairs with some empty.

One player is called Buffy, stands in the center, and is blindfolded while everyone else sits.

All players exchange seats.

The Master of Revels claps to begin the game.

Buffy steps in front of a chair and uses their knees to determine if someone is sitting in it.

They ask the sitter three questions.

Sitter answers in a disguised voice. They do not need to be intelligible or truthful in their answers.

After all questions are answered, Buffy guesses who the sitter is.

If Buffy guesses wrong, they go to another chair. If Buffy is right, the sitter goes to the center and becomes Buffy.

Guessing wrong earns a forfeit.

The Master of Revels ensures that nobody cheats by looking through the blindfold, touching the player, or changing seats when not allowed.

BUFFY WITH A STICK

A player is designated Buffy, they are blindfolded and given a small stick-like object or "wand."

The group forms a circle around Buffy.

The group hold hands and forms a circle around Buffy, singing, humming, and dancing around.

After going one complete round, the group stops.

Buffy then extends the wand. Whatever player the wand is pointing at, steps forward into the center of the circle and grabs hold of the other end of the wand.

Buffy asks the player holding the wand three questions.

They answer only in grunts, growls, or moans.

After all questions are "answered," Buffy guesses who the player is.

If right, the other player becomes Buffy.

If wrong, they owe a forfeit and must point their wand to pick a new player.

Buffy continues blindfolded until they correctly guess a

player or someone volunteers to take their place. If a volunteer takes their place, Buffy must pay a forfeit.

THE JINGLING MATCH

This game was more commonly played at country fairs for a set prize. It has been slightly adapted for a game night.

One player is the jingler. The jingler has a small bell in each hand.

Everyone but the jingler is blindfolded.

A timer is started. Depending on the size of the room or playing area, this can be thirty seconds to five minutes.

The jingler must continuously ring the bells during the game while avoiding being captured by the other players. The jingler cannot leave the room of the designated playing area to escape being captured.

If the jingler is caught, they must pay a forfeit.

HOT COCKLES

Two players are chosen.

Player one sits in a chair.

Player two is blindfolded, kneels before player one, puts

their head in player one's lap, and their hands behind their back.

The rest of the players take turns tapping the kneeling player. In most versions the taps are limited to player two's hands.

The kneeling player attempts to guess who has touched them.

Any player that is successfully identified must pay a forfeit.

If player two cannot identify anyone, they must pay a forfeit.

Guessing Games

These games all require guessing in some manner.

SHADOW BUFF

Set up a sheet or screen on one side of the room or use a white wall.

Shine a light on the screen so that people passing in front of it cast a shadow. Use candles for the authentic Regency experience.

A guesser is chosen and sits with their back to the light, so they can see the shadows cast but not who is casting them.

The first player casts a shadow. They are encouraged to distort it to hide their identity.

The guesser gets one guess of who the shadow belongs to.

If they are correct, the shadow caster gets a forfeit and becomes the guesser.

The game continues until everyone has a chance to cast a shadow.

THE PRISONER

A player is chosen to be the prisoner and another one is the accuser; everyone else are the judges.

The rest of the players are seated in a semi-circle.

The prisoner is seated at the other end of the room.

The accuser steps before the prisoner and says: "Most potent grave and revered judges know ye for what offence this prisoner is put to the bar to take his trial."

Each judge writes down what crime they think was committed.

The accuser takes the papers and reads them in a mixed-up order.

The prisoner must guess which crime belongs to which Judge.

If the prisoner guesses correctly, the judge earns a forfeit.

If the prisoner does not guess any judge correctly, they pay three forfeits.

The new prisoner is the first judge that was guessed correctly.

If the accuser gives any hints to the prisoner, they must pay a forfeit and become the prisoner.

MUSICAL MAGIC

One person is the guesser and is sent out of the room.

The remaining players determine an action the guesser should perform with an object in the room.

The guesser is allowed back into the room and music is played. Traditionally a piano or other instrument would be used, but you might use a recording.

The music gets louder when the guesser gets closer to doing the task and softer when he gets further.

When the guesser approaches the person or object that is involved in his task, the music will get louder. When the guesser touches the person or object, the music stops to let them know they have discovered some part of their task.

Then the guesser must try various actions. The music gets louder when they get closer to doing the right action.

If the guesser gives up or cannot figure out their action in a certain amount of time, then they must pay a forfeit.

For example, the task might be to kiss a lady's hand. The music would get louder as the guesser approached the lady. The music would stop when they touched the lady. As they reached for the lady's hand, the music would get louder. When they touched their hand, the music would stop. If they shook their hand, the music would get quieter. If they bow over the hand, the music would get louder. When they kissed the hand, the music would stop.

How entertaining this game is depends on the type of actions that are assigned to the guesser. It's important it not be too complicated or too simple.

THE THREE KINGDOMS

One person is the guesser and is sent out of the room.

The remaining players determine a word the guesser must guess.

The guesser returns to the room. They are allowed to ask six questions to try and divine the word. They can ask any of the other players their questions. Players must answer honestly.

The first question should ask which kingdom the word belongs to. The Three Kingdoms are Animal, Vegetable, or Mineral. An item may be one kingdom or a combination of kingdoms. For example, a silk fan is both Mineral and Animal.

If the guesser fails to name the word, they pay a forfeit. Any player who answers their question incorrectly will also pay a forfeit.

Note For Writers

In addition to providing lots of opportunities for touching, these games can be used to reveal things about your characters and their relationships. Games like The Prisoner rely on the players to know each other and deduce others' answers. A couple's compatibility or awareness of each other could be suggested through such a game.

Kissing Games

The Regency era had strict rules of conduct between men and women. Parlor games gave them a chance to bend the rules. Most of the "games" seem like thinly veiled excuses to kiss.

These kisses were not necessarily on the lips. Players could blow a kiss, kiss a hand, or kiss a cheek. As you will see in the Crying Forfeits section, many penances also involve kissing. This is only a small sampling of the kissing games I found.

THE POSTMAN

A "postman" stands outside the room and knocks.

The door is answered and the postman is asked if they have a letter and how many pennies it will cost.

The postman replies that they do have a letter and gives a name and number for the pennies.

The named player joins the postman outside the room and must kiss the postman as many times as the number given.

The player then becomes the next postman.

KISS THE MONKEY

A gentleman and lady kneel back-to-back with elbows intertwined. The lady looks over her left shoulder. The gentleman looks over his right shoulder.

He attempts to kiss her and she evades him by leaning away. If he succeeds before time has elapsed, then she pays a forfeit.

A VOYAGE TO CYPRESS

One player is declared the Bridegroom and another the Conductor.

The bridegroom chooses a lady to be the bride and they leave the room.

According to the book from 1822 while they are out of the room, "...if he does not give her a kiss he must be set down for a booby."

When they return to the room the conductor asks, "Where have you been?"

The bridegroom replies, "To Cypress to get married and only guess of what I made my bride a present."

Their "bride" then whispers to the conductor an article of clothing. For example, a bonnet.

Each lady is then asked to whisper their guess to the conductor. If they are wrong, then they must pay a forfeit or allow the bridegroom to kiss them.

The gentlemen then whisper their answers. If they are wrong, they pay a forfeit. The man who guesses correctly may kiss the bride.

Active Games

These games should be played in a large room or outside., as they need lots of space. Considered a way to "afford excellent exercise."

MOVE ALL

Chairs are arranged in a circle as far apart from each other as possible. There should be one less chair than the number of players.

One player is the caller and stands in the center. They say "Move All."

Every person must rise and change seats.

The person left standing pays a forfeit, and becomes the new caller.

No player is allowed to hold another player back, prevent them from reaching a seat, or pull them off their seat. If such delinquencies occur, the cheaters must pay a forfeit.

If a player does not change seats, they must pay two forfeits.

The quicker this game is played, the better.

THE TRENCHER

This is traditionally played with a wooden trencher (a large plate or bowl).

A circle of chairs is set up with one less chair than the number of players.

One player is the caller and stands in the middle of the circle holding the trencher. All the other players sit in the chairs.

Each player chooses a new name, the sillier the better.

The caller calls a name and throws the trencher into the air.

The player whose name is called must catch the trencher before it falls to the ground. If they don't, they must pay a forfeit.

The caller tries to sit in the called player's seat. If they fail, they pay a forfeit and must call again.

If they succeed, the called player becomes the caller.

Forfeits are also earned if the caller says the wrong name, or if any player stands when their name isn't called.

The caller can also call "Move All." This means every player must change seats. Any player that doesn't change seats or is left standing must pay a forfeit.

THE TOILETTE

Each player chooses a new name. It must be something used for toilette. For example, comb, mirror, powder puff, hairpin, rouge, etc.

The group is seated in a circle with a player standing in the middle called Lord or Lady Order.

The Lord/Lady will call for an item. For example: "My Lady wants her comb."

The player who is the comb must give their seat to Lady/Lord Order. The comb now becomes the lady and the lady becomes the comb.

The "spirit of the game depends upon the rapidity with which it is played."

The player who loses their seat must quickly name another object.

Anyone who does not jump up at their item or forgets their name must pay a forfeit.

The faster the game is played, the more forfeits will be paid.

THE WOLF AND DEER

"This game is most amusing when played in a garden or field."

The ladies choose a player to be the "Deer." In the Regency they would often choose a matron for this position.

One male player is chosen to be the "Wolf."

The deer stands and the rest of the ladies line up behind her. They make up her "tail."

The wolf starts the game by saying, "I am a wolf and one who is determined to devour you."

The deer says, "I am a deer not easily alarmed. It shall cost you dear, I promise you, if you attempt to put your threat in execution."

The wolf replies: "Well, if I can't eat your head at least I'll make free with a joint of your tail."

The wolf then tries to seize the last lady in line. The deer spreads her arms and tries to keep the wolf away from the tail.

The last lady in the line tries to avoid the wolf. The line must move with her. She tries to get in front of the deer before the wolf captures her.

If the wolf doesn't capture her then he pays a forfeit and a new wolf is chosen.

If the wolf captures the lady, then she pays a forfeit and sits down.

BULLET PUDDING

This game can get a little messy so play it on a hard, easily-cleaned surface.

Fill a large dish or bowl with flour.

Flip the bowl so the flour forms a dome.

Lay a coin or other small metal object at the top.

Each player cuts a slice out of the peaked flour.

The player who causes the bullet to fall from its place and into the flour must retrieve it.

They must pull the bullet out of the flour using their mouth or their chin, but not their hands.

If they do not retrieve the bullet, they must pay a forfeit.

Word Games

In the Regency, being clever with language was the mark of an intelligent person. Often games were designed around allowing the players to showcase their wordplay. I have omitted word games that might prove too complicated for a casual evening with those unused to such verbal tricks.

SHORT ANSWERS

Everyone sits in a circle, alternating gender.

A lady starts the game by asking the person on her right a question.

The question must be answered with a one syllable word.

After answering the question, the next player asks the player on their right a question.

None of the questions or answers can be repeated.

A forfeit is paid for every extra syllable in an answer, or whenever a question or answer is repeated.

Example Game

1st Lady: Permit me sir to ask if you love music?
1st Gent: Yes. Pray madam, do you like cold weather?
2nd L: No. Pray sir, are you not romantic?
2nd G: Yea. Pray madam, what wood do you think the best for making loggerheads?
3rd L: Oak. Pray sir, how d'ye do?
3rd G: Well. Have you much of the flint in your composition?
4th L: None. What must poor woman do to avoid herself spoken ill of?
5th G: Die. What sort of a man do you think I am?
6th L: Mad. What kind of people do you think prosper most in the world?
6th G: Fools.

THE FIVE VOWELS

"This game is rather an exercise of the mind than of the body but if conducted with ability will yield both mirth and entertainment."

The group sits in a circle.

The game is begun with one person asking a question of the person on their right.

Answers should make sense, be brief, and given promptly.

The questioner indicates what vowel must be omitted from the answer.

For example: Do you love apples? Answer me without an 'e.'

Suitable answers might be: "I don't" or "Fruit is always good."

Wrong answers would include "Yes," or "I really like them," since each of those responses includes the letter 'e.'

The player must answer the question or earn a forfeit.

Sometimes questions must be answered in clever ways. For example, if the answer to the question is four but the answer cannot contain the letter 'u', then they might answer "Five less one."

If a player answers using the vowel, they must pay a forfeit.

I LOVE MY LOVE WITH AN A

Traditionally this game is played orally, but modern players might enjoy writing down the words instead.

Players are each given a letter of the alphabet. X, Y, and Z are usually omitted.

They must complete the following phrase using only words that begin with that letter.

> I love my love with a (letter they are assigned), because she is _____. I hate her because she is_____.
> I took her to _____ to the sign of the _____. I treated her with _____ and her name is _____ _____ (two words both beginning with the letter).

Example

I love my love with an **A**, because she is **ardent**. I hate her because she is **ambitious**. I took her to **Andover** to the sign of the **Angel**. I treated her with **artichokes** and her name is **Anna Adair**.

A forfeit is paid for any blank the player cannot fill. Any player prompting another also receives a forfeit.

If the game is played long enough and all the letters have been used, a letter might be given again. But any player repeating a word already said must pay a forfeit.

This game can be made more difficult with a longer phrase.

I love my love with a (letter) because she is _____. I hate her because she is _____. By way of presents I gave her _____ (list four items). I took her to _____ to the sign of the _____ and treated her with _____ (list five items). Her name is _____ _____ (two words both beginning with the letter) and she is dressed in _____.

QUESTIONS AND RESPONSES

Unlike other games, the entire point of this one is to make each other laugh. There are no forfeits given.

This game will require the use of paper or note cards.

Each player gets two cards and a pen or pencil.

On one card they write a question and on the other a phrase that could be used to answer a variety of questions.

The question and answer should NOT match.

All players turn in their cards. A stack of questions and a stack of answers is created.

One stack is passed to the ladies and one stack to the gentlemen.

The first gentleman pulls the top question card and reads it aloud.

The first lady pulls the top answer card and reads it aloud.

Examples

Q: Do you have a lover?

A: Occasionally.

Q: Are you a wit?

A: That is a secret to all the world.

Crying Forfeits

Let a lady's bonnet be kept for the purpose of holding their deposits and a gentleman's hat for those of the Cavaliers. Whenever a forfeit is incurred the party must simply furnish a small cord or slip of paper on which his or her name is written thus no possible mistakes can arise and it will be no longer necessary for a fair hand to be stript of all its rings, ears of their pendants, and necks of their collars... while the poor Cavaliers after having surrendered their watches, snuff boxes, pen knives, and pencil cases are like inveterate drunkards reduced to the necessity of pawning even the very garments from their backs.

— WINTER EVENING PASTIMES

From reading the primary sources, it seems the point of playing parlor games is to accumulate forfeits. Some of the suggested penances I found were complicated and would take more time than a game. I tried to provide both short and long penances in my list of suggestions.

The key to a hilarious round of Crying Forfeits is in using

a combination of intelligence, wit, and knowledge of the individual players. The penance should match the abilities and personalities of the person. Get creative with the penances that are owed, but remember that they should not be demeaning or uncomfortable for any players. The goal is for everyone to laugh and enjoy the silliness, not to be embarrassed. Any kissing penance does not need to be paid with kisses on the lips. Air kisses, cheek kisses, or hand kisses are perfectly acceptable.

HOW IT WORKS

Throughout the games, the Mistress or Master of the Revels will keep track of the forfeits, either in a hat, as suggested above, on a scoring sheet, or another method.

After completing the last game of the evening the mistress or master will say, "Cry Forfeits."

She will then select an individual to pay their penance. This could be done by drawing their forfeits from the hat or a similar random method.

She says: "A forfeit I've here lost in fair game." She then names the penance required to redeem the forfeit.

Penances need not be played one at a time. One player may be instructed not to laugh for five minutes, another told to stand in a corner, and another to repeat tongue twisters. Multiple players may pay their penances in a group task.

The mistress or master will ensure that all forfeits are paid before the party breaks up for the evening.

Suggested Penances

I cannot imagine why you should refuse to lend your countenance to a little inoffensive kissing. It well becomes indeed a parcel of frumps to be so squeamish about a privilege by which they are themselves the greatest gainers since but for these games of forfeits many an old maid would leave the world with cheeks unsmacked by the two lips of mortal man.

— WINTER EVENING PASTIMES

KISSING PENANCES

Running the Gauntlet

The gentlemen form two lines facing each other. The lady paying her penance must walk between the gentlemen. Each one may demand a kiss as the price of passage. The penance is paid when the lady reaches the end of the line.

Kissing by Measure

The player takes a ribbon or piece of string and ties a knot in the middle. They choose another player and both place an end in their mouth. They nibble on their ends until they reach the knot. Their lips meeting ends the forfeit. The chosen player may drop their end but the penitent may not.

Fishing for a Kiss

A grape is tied to a piece of thread tied to a pen. The grape is hung before the player paying penance. The player must take the grape into their mouth and allow themselves to be led about the room. The "fisherman" will cry out what a fine fish they have caught. They can then detach the thread from the pen and put it in their own mouth, approaching the player until their lips meet.

Q in the Corner

The player is ordered into the corner. Other players may approach and ask, "What's the use of being sulky; come give me a kiss and be friends." If the player does not prefer the speaker they turn away and bids them begone. If they favor the speaker, they may salute them with a kiss and be led back to their seat.

Kiss Who You Love Best

The player is commanded to kiss who they love best. To avoid revealing their feelings, they might need to kiss every man/woman in the room.

Kiss Your Shadow

A player must kiss the spot where their shadow falls. They

may try and get their shadow to fall on a particular someone so they might kiss them.

Kiss the Candlestick

A lady attempts to kiss a candlestick held by a gentleman. The gentleman would move the candlestick, often putting himself in the way of her lips.

COMICAL PENANCES

The Confessional

The player paying penance sits in the middle of the room and is interrogated with ridiculous questions that they must answer but they're encouraged to be equally ridiculous. Example: Is there anyone you love better than yourself?

Care must be taken not to give offense with the questions.

Comparisons

The player is requested to compare a lady or gentleman to an object and explain how they resemble it and how they differ. This can be a clever way to compliment.

"A gentleman compares a lady to a chimney clock. Like that article of furniture, she ornaments the room wherein she is placed but unlike it makes us forget the hours as they fly instead of calling attention to them."

The Perfect Woman (or Man)

The player describes their perfect woman or man by selecting qualities of the other guests. All these admirable qualities are to be combined into an imaginary individual. For example if you were playing with my critique partners you might say, "The perfect woman would have the wit of Karen, the kindness of Whitney, and the humor of Cindy."

The Hobby Horse

The penitent player gets on their hands and knees and must carry another player about the room so they can be saluted (kissed) by the other players. "This will be found amusing to the company and encouraging to trade in the matter of dress trousers."

The Sofa

The penitent gets on their hands and knees and a couple sits upon them and exchanges a kiss.

SHORT PENANCES

Bow to the wittiest, kneel to the prettiest, and kiss who they love best.
Imitate animals named by the rest of the players without laughing.
Don't laugh for five minutes no matter what the other players do or say.
Give advice, useful or ridiculous, to a set number of players.
Create a rhyme to a line given by a player.

Cry in one corner, laugh in another, and sing in a third.
Lie down on the floor and rise with their arms folded.
Repeat a tongue twister designated by the other players.
Yawn until someone else in the room also yawns.
Stand on a chair and pose according to the directions.
Sing a verse from a song.
Remain silent for five minutes.
Count backward from 100.
Submit to being tickled for several minutes.
Recite a passage of poetry or from a play.
Tell a good story or joke.
Whisper a secret to one or more players.
Pay compliments to specific members of the party.

Use your creativity to come up with your own!

Additional Resources

...a fondness for reading, which, properly directed, must be an education in itself.

— MANSFIELD PARK

Literature

REFERENCED BY JANE AUSTEN

―⁂―

The following are mentioned by Austen in her books or personal correspondence and would be suitable for reading aloud. Free copies can be found online through Google Books or Project Gutenberg. For a complete index, visit pemberley.com.

NOVELS OR MEMOIRS

A Journey from London to Genoa by Joseph Baretti
A Sentimental Journey Through France and Italy by Laurence Sterne
Belinda by Maria Edgeworth
Camilla, or a Picture of Youth by Frances Burney
Cecilia, or Memoirs of an Heiress by Frances Burney
The Italian by Ann Radcliffe
Journal of the Embassy to China by Lord Macartney
The Monk by Matthew Gregory Lewis

The Mysteries of Udolpho by Ann Radcliffe
Paradise Lost by John Milton
Patronage by Maria Edgeworth
Robinson Crusoe by Daniel Defoe
The Romance of the Forest by Ann Radcliffe
The Vicar of Wakefield by Oliver Goldsmith
Waverly by Sir Walter Scott

PLAYS

Bon Ton or High Life Above Stairs by David Garrick
Hamlet by William Shakespeare
Henry the Eighth by William Shakespeare
Lovers' Vows by Mrs. Inchbald
A Midsummer's Night Dream by William Shakespeare
Much Ado About Nothing by William Shakespeare
The Rivals by Richard Brinsley Sheridan
Romeo and Juliet by William Shakespeare
Twelfth Night by William Shakespeare

ANTHOLOGIES

Arabian Nights Entertainments
Elegant Extracts: Or, Useful and Entertaining Pieces of Poetry by Vicesimus Knox

ESSAYS

The Idler by Samuel Johnson
Sermons to Young Women by James Fordyce
On Picturesque Beauty; On Picturesque Travel; and On

Sketching Landscape: to which is Added a Poem, On Landscape Painting by William Gilpin

POETRY

The Bride of Abydos by Lord Byron
The Corsair by Lord Byron
Elegy to the Memory of an Unfortunate Lady by Alexander Pope
Essay on Criticism by Alexander Pope
The Giaour by Lord Byron
Henry and Emma by Matthew Prior
The Hermit by James Beattie
Lady of the Lake by Sir Walter Scott
Marmion by Sir Walter Scott
The Sofa by William Cowper
Spring by Thomson
Tales by George Crabbe
Truth by William Cowper
The Winter Evening by William Cowper

Recommended Short Poems

It is sometimes forgotten that Jane Austen lived at the same time as the Romantic poets. Like Austen's work, their poetry is still popular today and will be familiar to your party guests. For a short poetry reading, I recommend the following. If nobody wants to read aloud, you can find all of these on YouTube (sometimes read by a celebrity).

A Red, Red Rose by Robert Burns
Bright star! would I were steadfast as thou art by John Keats
Composed upon Westminster Bridge by William Wordsworth
The day is gone, and all its sweets are gone! by John Keats
Frost at Midnight by Samuel Taylor Coleridge
I Wandered Lonely as A Cloud by William Wordsworth
Kubla Khan by Samuel Taylor Coleridge
London by William Blake
Sonnet on being Cautioned against Walking on a Headland by Charlotte Smith
The Tyger by William Blake

Music

SHEET MUSIC

For those with the patience and the ability it would be possible to play the exact same music that Jane Austen enjoyed at home. Like many others during the Regency, the Austen family maintained personal collections of music. Thanks to the University of Southampton, the Austen family music books have been digitized and are available online through The Internet Archive. There are nearly six hundred pieces of music available for view at. https://archive.org/details/austenfamilymusicbooks

If you don't wish to search through the digitized books, you might pick any of the composers who were popular during the Regency. Here is a brief list:

Charles Dibdin

Franz Schubert
George Fredrick Handel
Ignaz Pleyel
Joseph Haydn
Ludwig van Beethoven
Luigi Boccherini
Samuel Webbe the Younger
Wolfgang Amadeus Mozart

RECORDED MUSIC

Most of us won't be able to play a sonata or even own a piano. Luckily, over the years several professional musicians have recorded songs from the Regency. Some collections are specific to the Austen family music books and others just true to the period. The following albums provide a good variety. They are all available on various music streaming services or as a CD.

Amusing Aunt Jane by Lisa Timbs (only available via her website thesquarepianist.co.uk)
The Era of Jane Austen (Music of the Late 18th-Early 19th Century) by Countdown Media
The Jane Austen Collection by Divine Art Ltd
The Jane Austen Companion by Nimbus Records
Jane Austen Entertains by The Gift of Music
The Jane Austen Era by Cobra Entertainment
Jane Austen Piano Favorites by The Gift of Music
Jane Austen's Songbook by Albany Records

BUILDING A PLAYLIST

Using the music from the above albums you can build your perfect Regency party playlist. Most of the instrumental music is suitable for background ambiance. I would recommend having a moment when the party can appreciate a vocal performance or two. I love The Highland Laddie on The Jane Austen Collection album. It is a fun song but my love for it mostly stems from its use in the 2009 BBC adaptation of Emma.

Recipes

"By the bye, Charles, are you really serious in meditating a dance at Netherfield?—I would advise you, before you determine on it, to consult the wishes of the present party; I am much mistaken if there are not some among us to whom a ball would be rather a punishment than a pleasure."

"If you mean Darcy," cried her brother, "he may go to bed, if he chuses, before it begins—but as for the ball, it is quite a settled thing; and as soon as Nicholls has made white soup enough I shall send round my cards."

— PRIDE AND PREJUDICE

White Soup

This recipe is adapted from John Farley's *London Art of Cooking (1783)*. Mr. Bingley would have served something similar at the Netherfield Ball.

INGREDIENTS

    2 soup bones with some meat (veal or beef bone)
    10 1/2 c. water
    2 chicken thighs
    1/2 lb bacon
    3/4 c. white rice
    1 anchovy or anchovy paste
    A few peppercorns
    Thyme, bay leaf, and parsley
    2 small/medium onions, roughly chopped
    2 ribs of celery, roughly chopped
    1/4 lb ground sugared almonds
    1 c. thickened cream
    1 egg yolk

Using a large saucepan, simmer the bones, water, chicken, bacon, rice, anchovies, peppercorns, herbs, onions, and celery for two hours on low.
Strain through a sieve into another large pot.
Let sit overnight in the refrigerator.
Skim the fat off the top.
Add the almonds and bring to boil.
Strain again to remove the almond pieces.
Mix together the egg yolk and cream in a small bowl and stir into the soup.

Chicken Salad

This recipe was originally found in the 1808 book *A New System of Domestic Cookery* and was adapted by Jennifer Stanley. More of her recipes can be found on her website: savoringthepast.net.

INGREDIENTS
- 3/4 lb of roasted chicken, completely cooled
- 2-3 anchovies
- 1 chopped shallot
- 3/4 c. parsley
- 1 tbsp olive or almond oil
- 2 tbsp lemon juice
- 2 tbsp distilled vinegar
- 1 tsp mustard
- Salt and pepper to taste

Mince anchovies and combine with shallots and parsley.
In a separate bowl mix: oil, lemon juice, vinegar, mustard, salt

and pepper and whisk together. Then add to the anchovy mix. Stir well.
Shred chicken and add to the vinaigrette.
Completely coat the chicken.
Cover the bowl and set in the refrigerator for two to three hours.

Serve on toast for historical accuracy.

Negus

This is the basic, classic negus recipe that was often served at Regency balls. No doubt individual cooks had their own unique twists. You might choose to experiment by adding more spices. Cloves, ginger, licorice, or coriander have all been listed in some negus recipes.

INGREDIENTS
- 2 c port wine*
- 4 c water
- 1 c sugar
- 1 lemon
- Ground nutmeg to taste

Zest and juice lemon.
Add sugar, nutmeg, lemon juice, and zest to the wine.
Boil the water and add it to the wine mixture.
Cover and let cool.
Serve.

*While port was the most common wine used, sherry or any other sweet white wine may be substituted. For non-alcoholic versions replace wine with apple or cranberry juice.

Syllabub

> His heart, which (to use your favourite comparison) was as delicate as sweet and as tender as a Whipt-syllabub, could not resist her attractions…
>
> — LESLEY CASTLE, BY JANE AUSTEN, 1792

These are basic recipes adapted from the Jane Austen Centre and the Colonial Williamsburg websites. Feel free to adjust the ratio between cream and liquid to change the consistency.

Modern appliances can keep the syllabub cold but traditionally it would be left at room temperature. It was generally served after the cream and liquid separated.

Using these two recipes as a base, you can experiment with other flavors by adding pureed fruit or flavored syrups.

WHIPT LEMON SYLLABUB

Ingredients
2 c. whipped heavy cream

1/2 c. white sugar
1/8 c white wine or lemon juice
1/8 c freshly-squeezed lemon juice and zest of lemon
Grated nutmeg
Sprig of mint
Lemon slices

Whip cream in a chilled bowl. As the cream starts to thicken, add sugar, white wine, lemon juice, and zest.
Whip until thick.
Chill in the refrigerator until ready to serve.
This will be thick enough to eat with a spoon.
Serve with a garnish of mint, lemon slice, and nutmeg. Makes ten servings.

SOLID NON-ALCOHOLIC SYLLABUB

INGREDIENTS
2 c. heavy whipping cream
2 c. apple juice
1 lemon
2 tbsp. sugar or to taste

Grate the lemon peel and then juice the lemon.
Add cream, apple juice, and lemon juice into a large plastic container with a sealable top.
Shake until the sound changes from sloshing to muffled.
Open and taste. If more sweetness is desired, add sugar. Some apple juice may be sweet enough that no additional sugar will be needed.
Pour mixture into serving glasses and let sit until cream and liquid separate.
Can be served at room temperature or chilled.

Ices

ICE CREAM AND SORBET

She was a little shocked at the want of two drawing rooms, at the poor attempt at rout-cakes, and there being no ice in the Highbury card parties.

— EMMA

These basic recipes for Regency ices leave room for creativity. For different flavors, add jams, syrups, or pureed fruit to the recipe. Try your hand at some of the more unusual ones, like jasmine or eggplant. To really give your ice that period feel, freeze them in a molded shape.

LEMON ICE CREAM

INGREDIENTS
- 1 lemon
- 2/3 c. sugar
- 7 tbsp. fresh lemon juice
- 2 ½ c. heavy cream
- 1 c. milk

5 egg yolks

Zest the lemon. Put zest and sugar in a food processor until finely chopped.
Mix the lemon sugar with milk and 1 ½ cups of cream in a saucepan and bring to a boil.
Stir occasionally to help dissolve the sugar.
In a large bowl, whisk egg yolks. While whisking, slowly add the hot cream.
Once smooth, pour the mixture back into a saucepan or on top of a double boiler.
Cook over low heat, stirring constantly, until a thick custard (about 15 min). Do not let boil.
Place custard in a metal bowl set atop a larger bowl of ice.
Stir until very cold and thick.
Mix in lemon juice.*
Whip the remaining cream until stiff and fold into the custard.
Freeze in a shallow pan until partially set.
Scoop ice cream into a bowl and beat until smooth but not melted.
Return to freezer until solid in bowl or mold as desired.
Makes 1 quart.

SIMPLIFIED LEMON ICE

Ingredients

2 c. sugar
4 c. water
1 c. fresh lemon juice
2 tbsp lemon zest
Dash of salt

In a saucepan combine everything but the lemon juice.
Boil for five minutes. Then cool.

Once cooled, add lemon juice.*
Pour into a dish and cover. Freeze for at least six hours.
Break mixture into chunks and place in a food processor.
Process until smooth.
Makes 1/2 gallon.

*If making a different flavor, replace lemon juice with desired syrup, jam, or pureed fruit.

More Riddles

"I like your plan," cried Mr. Weston. "Agreed, agreed. I will do my best. I am making a conundrum. How will a conundrum reckon?"

— EMMA

Below I have included thirty-three more riddles for your enjoyment. Even more word puzzles can be found in *A Choice Collection of Riddles, Charades, Rebusses* by Peter Puzzlewell. Or you could examine the massive collection in *Guess Me: A Curious Collection of Enigmas, Charades, Acting Charade, Double Acrostics, Conundrums, Verbal Puzzles, Hieroglyphics, Anagrams, etc.* Both are available online via The Internet Archive or Google Books, although it is important to note that *Guess Me* was published in 1879 and so is not Regency but Victorian.

HOLLI JO MONROE

RIDDLES

Riddle 6
Although a human shape I wear
Mother I never had
And though no sense nor life I share
In finest silks I'm clad
By ev'ry miss I'm valued much
Belov'd and highly priz'd
Yet still my cruel fate is such
By boys I am despis'd

Riddle 7
With monks and with hermits I chiefly reside
From courts and from camps at a distance
The ladies who ne'er could my presence abide
To banish me join their assistance
Though seldom I flatter I oft show respect
To the prelate the patriot and peer
But sometimes alas! a sad proof of neglect
Or a mark of contempt I appear
By the couch of the sick I am frequently found
And I always attend on the dead
With patient affliction I sit on the ground
But if talk'd of I'm instantly fled

Riddle 8
Sixteen adjectives, twenty-four pronouns, a disappointed lobster, an oyster in love, and nineteen radicals, may all be expressed in one common liquid.

Riddle 9
Native of Cashmire in each fragrant grove

I reign the pride and empress of the spring
And on my feast the black-eyed maidens love
The gay profusion of my buds to fling
These are the fair resemblances of youth
Which with its pleasures swiftly fade away
But my undying odor like firm truth
Nor suffers change nor ever knows decay

Riddle 10

Ever eating never cloying
All devouring all destroying
Never finding full repast
Till I eat the world at last

Riddle 11

I am not what I was, I am quite the reverse
I am what I was, which is still more perverse
From morning to night I do nothing but fret
With wishing to be what I never was yet

Riddle 12

Pray tell me, ladies, if you can
Who is that highly favour'd man
Who, though he marry many a wife
May still live single all his life?

Riddle 13

What is the longest and the shortest thing in the world? The swiftest and the slowest? The most indivisible and the most extended? The least valued and the most regretted? Without which nothing can be done? Which devours all that is small, yet gives life to all that is great?

Riddle 14

Before my birth I had a name
But soon as born I lost the same
And when I'm laid within the tomb
I shall my father's name assume
I change my name three days together
Yet live but one in any weather

Riddle 15

A valued emblem of distinguis'd place
A mimic brute with all but human face
A lion-hearted hero, fam'd of old
What makes the fiercest warrior's heart grow cold
A distant light th'initials will declare
What oft a pleasure proves and oft a snare

Riddle 16

Of heav'nly origin to earth I came
To solace human kind
The cement of each social frame
Balm to the wounded mind
So lov'd so valued through the world
That dark pretenders take
My form with colours false unfurl'd
For gain or mischief's sake

CONUNDRUMS

Conundrum 6
Why are good resolutions like fainting ladies?

Conundrum 7
When is coffee like the soil?

Conundrum 8
Why is a spectator like a bee-hive?

Conundrum 9
Why are sheep in a fold like a handsome letter?

Conundrum 10
Why is the letter F like Paris?

Conundrum 11
What is that which goes from London to York without once moving?

Conundrum 12
What is every thing doing at the same time?

Conundrum 13
What is the oldest tree?

Conundrum 14
Why is a lawyer like a tailor?

Conundrum 15
What is that, which, though blind itself, leads the blind?

Conundrum 16
Why is a lucky gambler an agreeable fellow?

CHARADES

Charade 6
My love for you shall never know my first; nor shall it be my second; but it shall be my whole.

Charade 7
My first is an heir, my second a snare.
My whole is the offspring of fancy,
Which I sent out of play, upon Valentine's day,
As a token of love to my Nancy.

Charade 8
My first is a substance that's light;
My second makes many things tight:
My whole is the key to delight.

Charade 9
My first does affliction denote,
Which my second is born to endure;
My whole is the best antidote
That affliction to soften or cure.

Charade 10
My first is a preposition;
My second a composition;
My whole an acquisition.

Charade 11
Some say my first is nothing, but I know
It has a meaning from the lips of woe;
My second you may take wide as you will,
O'er wilderness and garden, dale and hill;

Charade 12

My first is a place where no promises bind;
My second is toss'd by each wavering wind:
My whole is unstable as friendship or weather,
And those who trust to it rely on a feather.

Charade 13

My first the source of various good,
For man and beast supplying food;
My next results from cold or fear,
But quickly flies when aid is near:
My whole strikes terror to the heart,
And awful rends my first apart.

Charade 14

My first I would venture for;
My second I would venture in;
My whole is more talked of than practised.

Charade 15

My first is an obligation;
My second is inevitable:
My whole is a slavery.

Charade 16

When night brings on her noontide hour,
And stillness holds her magic power,
All mortals to my first repair,
And bid adieu to toil and care.
My next for various ends design'd,
Yet oft my first you there will find:
Within my whole you seek repose,
Forgetting life and all its woes.

More Riddle Answers

RIDDLES

6. Doll
7. Silence
8. Ink
9. Rose
10. Fire
11. Old Maid
12. Clergyman
13. Time
14. Today
15. Money
16. Friendship

CONUNDRUMS

6. They want carrying out.
7. When it is ground.
8. He is a be-holder.
9. They are well-penned.
10. Because it is the capital of France.
11. The road.
12. Growing older.
13. The elder tree.
14. Because he deals in suits.
15. A stick.
16. Because he has such winning ways.

CHARADES

6. Endless
7. Sonnet
8. Corkscrew
9. Woman
10. Fortune
11. Orange
12. Courtship
13. Earthquake
14. Friendship
15. Bondage
16. Bedroom

Enjoyed this book?

YOU CAN MAKE A DIFFERENCE!

In a world full of excellent entertainment, reviews are a powerful way to find readers. Every review counts! Honest reviews help others find my books. And the more readers I have the more books I will be able to write!

If you enjoyed *The Proper Guide to Parlor Games* I would be very grateful if you could spend a few minutes leaving a review. It can be as short as you like and would mean the world to me.

JOIN THE INNER CIRCLE NEWSLETTER

Get an exclusive printable scoring sheet and sample invitation!

Sign-Up at: https://tinyurl.com/hjparlor

The best part of being a writer is getting to connect with readers. I send occasional newsletters with updates on my writing, details on new releases, and fun freebies. No spam. Ever.

Acknowledgments

I always worry that in acknowledging some I will offend others, and yet it feels wrong not to thank those who have made this book possible.

I have to thank my parents, for their patience and support, my sister Marcee for pushing me to "do the thing", and all my siblings for not laughing at my dreams.

This book started as a fun little booklet and grew into so much more. For that I must thank my critique partners for encouraging me and pushing me to make this book a reality. Karen, Whitney, and Cindy you are the literal best.

I also want to thank my editor Julia Allen for catching all my slips and polishing the manuscript to a bright shine.

And finally to all my fellow Janeites out there, who love Austen and the Regency. Without your books, podcasts, blogs, and videos. I would never have wandered down this rabbit hole and made it my home.

About the Author

Holli Jo is a country girl who joined the Army and became a Captain before leaving the service to travel and pursue writing. She enjoys all genres as long as they have some romance. Naturally curious, she is full of random facts and loves to research. Holli Jo's survived live nerve agent training, deployed to Afghanistan, climbed Kilimanjaro, backpacked around the world, and SCUBA dived in Bali so she knows that sometimes staying home with a book is the best adventure of all.

To stay in the know, join the newsletter at hollijomonroe.com

facebook.com/AuthorHollijo
instagram.com/hollijo.writes

Selected Bibliography

Adkins, Roy, and Lesley Adkins. *Jane Austen's England: Daily Life in the Georgian and Regency Periods*. New York, New York: Penguin Books, 2014.

Allen, Louise. *Regency Slang Revealed*. Createspace Independent Publishing Platform, 2016.

Austen, Jane. *The Complete Works of Jane Austen (Including Novels, Personal Letters & Scraps)*. e-artnow, 2017.

Collingwood, Francis. *The Universal Cook, and City and Country Housekeeper. Containing All the Various Branches of Cookery ... Together with Directions for Baking Bread, the Management of Poultry and the Diary, and the Kitchen and Fruit Garden, Etc. [with Portraits.]*. R. Noble, 1792.

Davidson, Hilary. *Dress in the Age of Jane Austen. Regency Fashion*. New Haven: Yale University Press, 2019.

Evening Amusements; Or, a New Book of Games and Forfeits. London: Dean and Munday, 1828.

Frederick D'Arros Planché. *Guess Me: A Curious Collection of Enigmas, Charades, Acting Charades, Double Acrostics, ... Anagrams, Etc. ... Illustrated by G. Cruickshank and Others*, 1872.

Fullerton, Susannah. *A Dance with Jane Austen: How a Novelist and Her Characters Went to the Ball*. Minneapolis, Mn: Frances Lincoln Limited, 2012.

jasna.org. "Home» JASNA." Accessed November 15, 2022. https://jasna.org.

Hoyle, Edmond. *The New Pocket Hoyle*. Smith, 1810.

pemberley.com. "Jane Austen at the Republic of Pemberley," 2022. https://pemberley.com/.

Jane Austen Centre and the Jane Austen Online Gift Shop. "Jane Austen Centre and Jane Austen Online Gift Shop," n.d. https://janeausten.co.uk.

Mullan, John. *What Matters in Jane Austen?: Twenty Crucial Puzzles Solved*. New York: Bloomsbury Press, 2014.

Parlett, David. "Historic Card Games Described by David Parlett." www.parlettgames.uk, 2022. https://www.parlettgames.uk/histocs.

SELECTED BIBLIOGRAPHY

Puzzlewell, Peter. *A Choice Collection of Riddles, Charades, Rebusses, &C. Part Third*. E. Newbery, 1796.

Revel, Rachel. *Winter Evening Pastimes; Or, the Merry-Maker's Companion:* Alex. Mesnard, 1825.

Round Games for All Parties. S. French, 1800.

Stanley, Jennifer. "A 200-Year Old Chicken Salad Recipe." Savoring the Past, December 6, 2016. https://savoringthepast.net/2016/12/06/a-200-year-old-chicken-salad-recipe/.

Strutt, Joseph. *Glig Gamena Angel Deod, Or, the Sports and Pastimes of the People of England*. T. Bensley, for White and Company, 1801.

www.colonialwilliamsburg.org. "Syllabubs Three Ways." Accessed November 15, 2022. https://www.colonialwilliamsburg.org/learn/recipes/syllabubs/.

Taylor, Bryton. "White Soup | Pride and Prejudice." In Literature, July 16, 2017. https://www.inliterature.net/food-in-literature/main-meals/soup/2017/07/pride-and-prejudice-white-soup.html.

IMAGE CREDITS

All images are in the public domain and obtained from the following collections.

The Internet Archive
The Library of Congress
The Metropolitan Museum of Art
Minneapolis Institute of Art
National Library of France
National Library of Medicine
The New York Public Library
Wikimedia Commons
Yale Center for British Art

Made in the USA
Monee, IL
28 February 2023